Published by thesohobookie.com

ISBN-13: 978-1543222463
ISBN-10: 1543222463

contact: marilynhenrion@mac.com   www.edwardhenrion.com

Mickey Rat

a not-for-children book

by

Edward Henrion

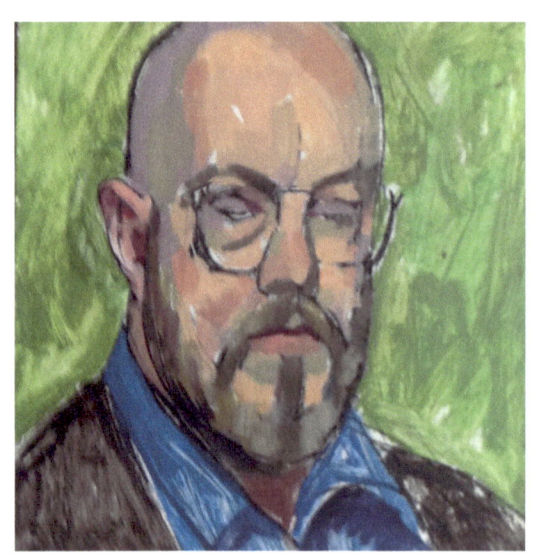

Edward Henrion 1928-2016

INTRODUCTION

Although not discovered until his death in 2016, the manuscript for this book was created by my late husband, Edward Henrion sometime in the 1970's or '80's. The content is just as relevant today. Political satire has a long and respected history throughout the world, and he was one of the true masters of this art form. Taking no prisoners, he was a sharp-eyed commentator on world events without regard to political-correctness.

Although he was a valued illustrator for publications such as *Human Events* and *Libertarian Review*, Edward otherwise eschewed a life in the spotlight and studiously avoided the "business of art" throughout his life. His satirical drawings remained hidden in his studio, not to see the light of day until he gave permission in 2011 to publish some of them in two books, *"Sweet and Lovely"* and *"Top Hat."* Even then, many of his works were still kept hidden, including this book.

The original book, as it was discovered, consisted of individual drawings and text pages that were enclosed in a hand-made folder with the cover page, all carefully wrapped in tissue paper and contained in a meticulously hand-made latched box. I do not know exactly when it was created, nor what (if any) plans he had for it. In spite of a close 64 year marriage, the mysteries of this extraordinary man continue to intrigue me.

The time has come to share them with the public.

Marilyn Henrion, March, 2017

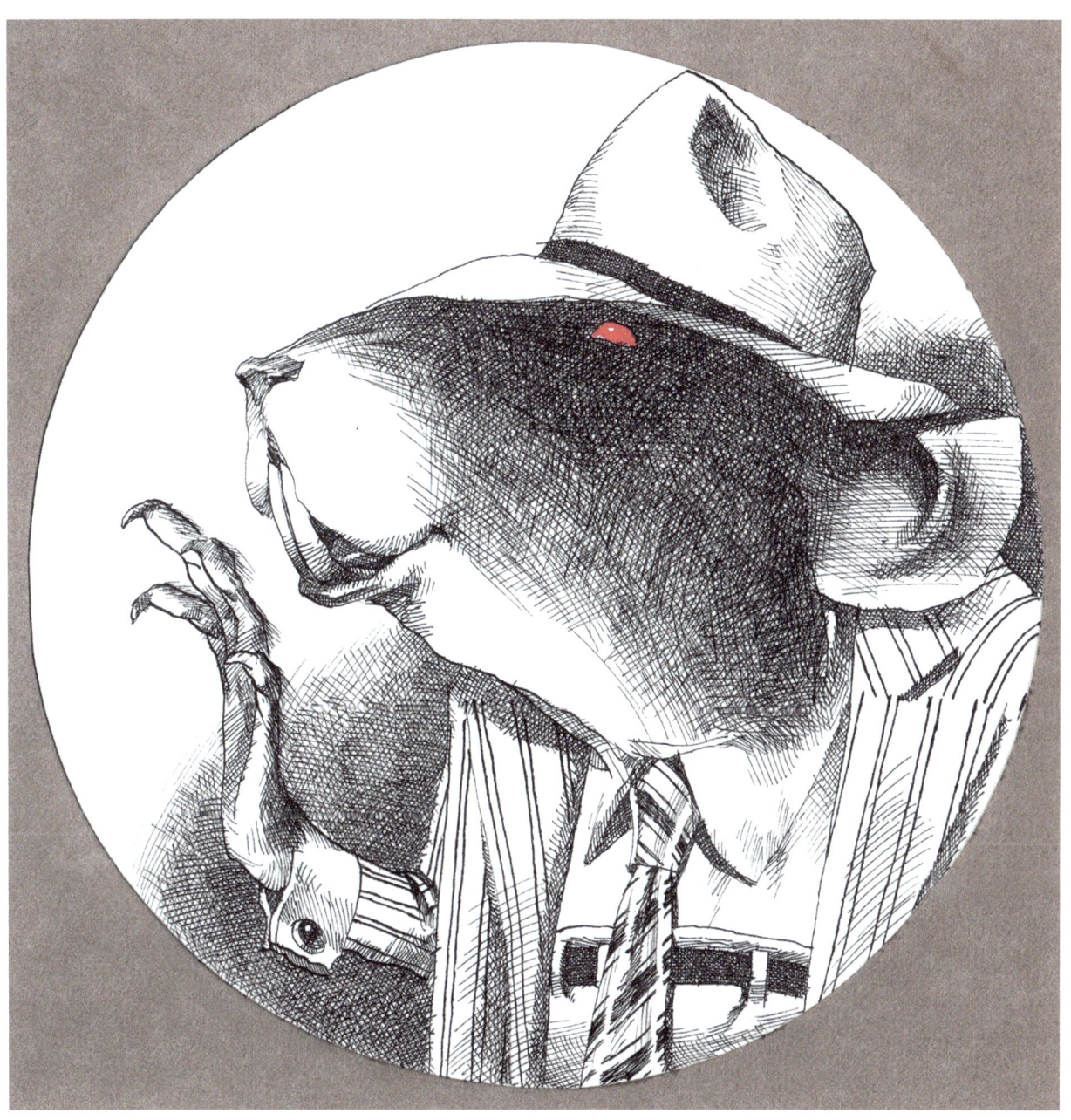

Hc came to the land
as a small rodent.
He had heard the roads
were paved with cheese.
They're not.

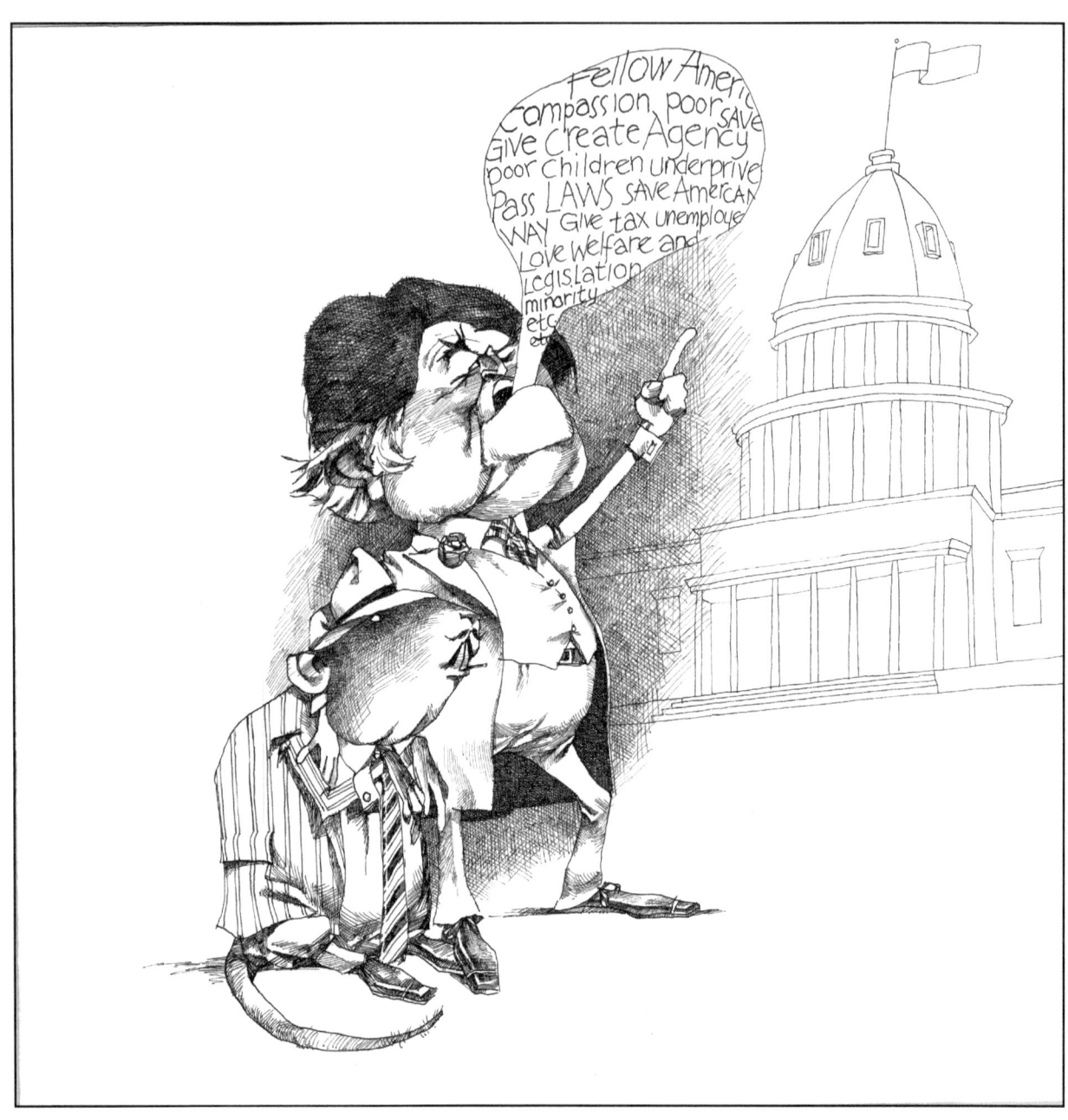

Politicians
clergy and lawyers
encouraged, blessed
and defended him, for naught.
He was a loser.

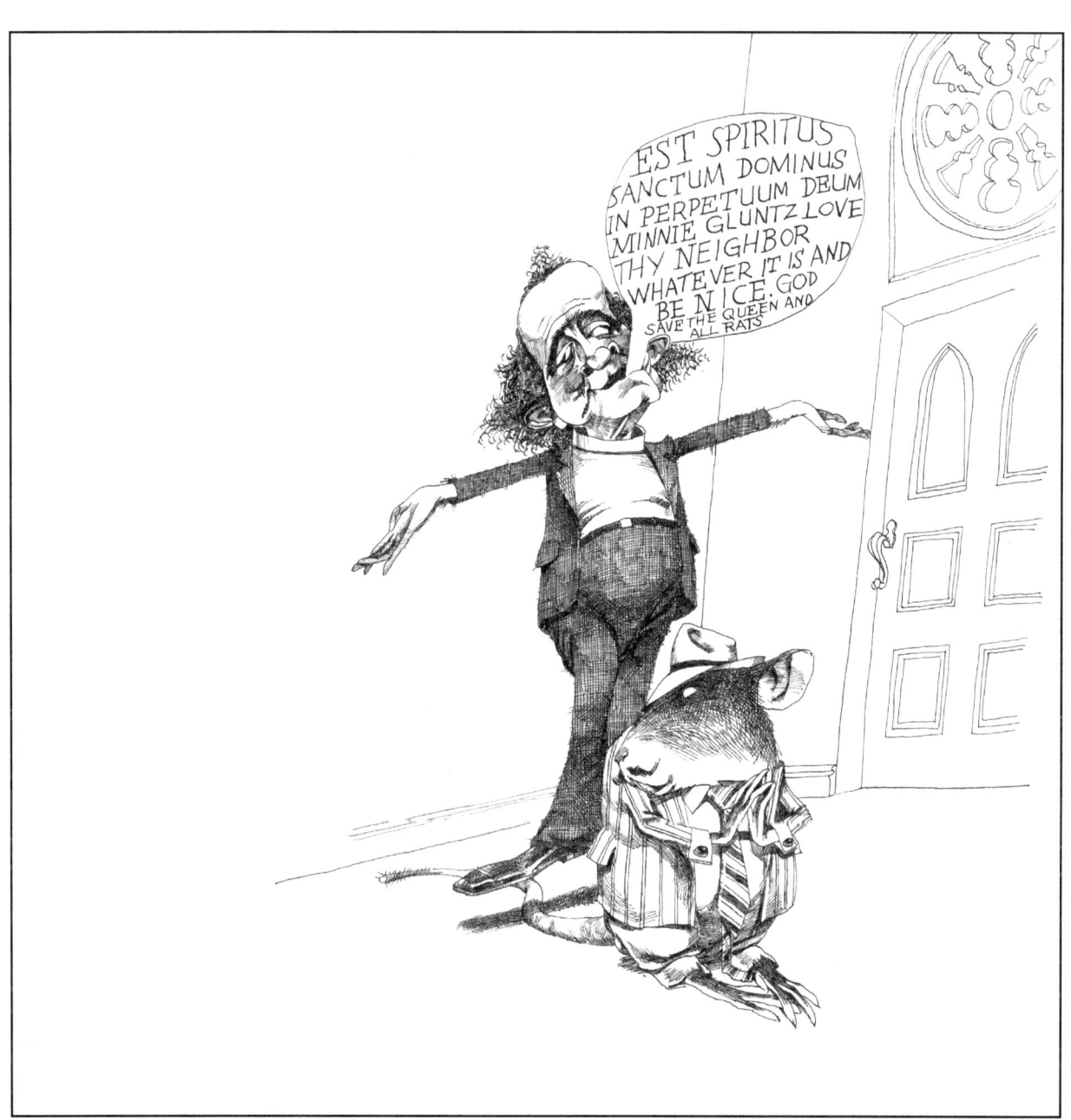

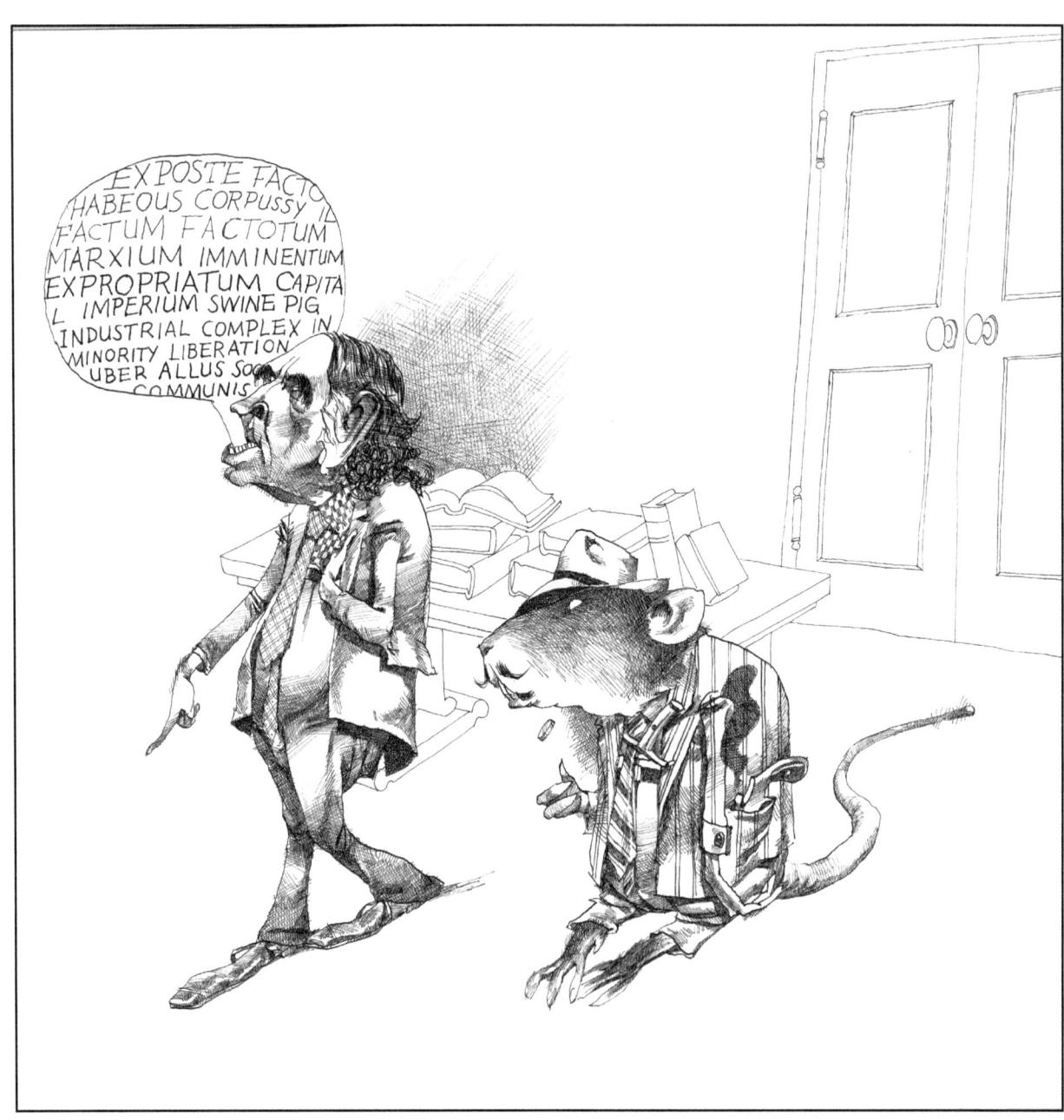

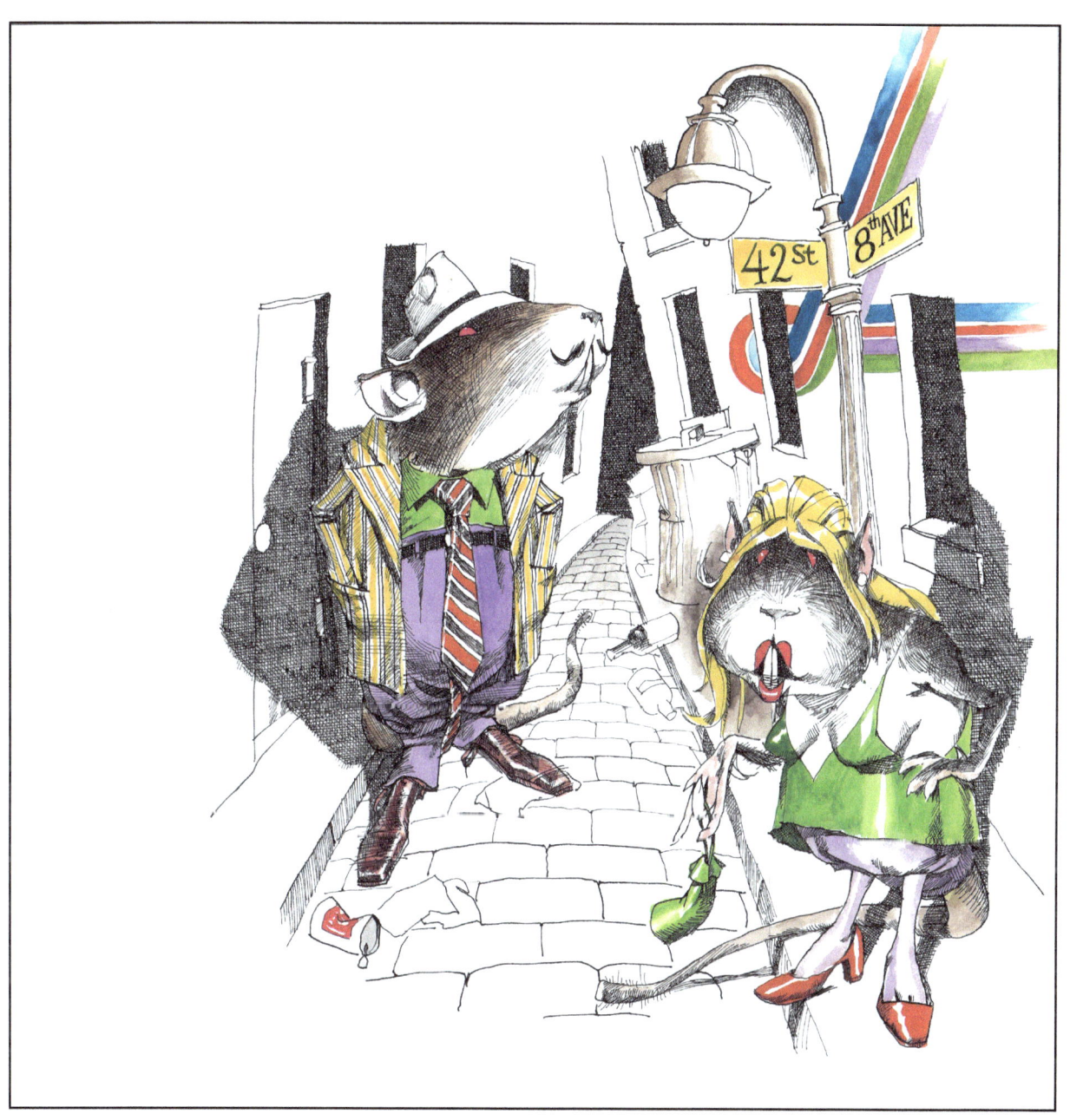

Mickey turned
to 42nd Street
for consolation,
met Minnie.

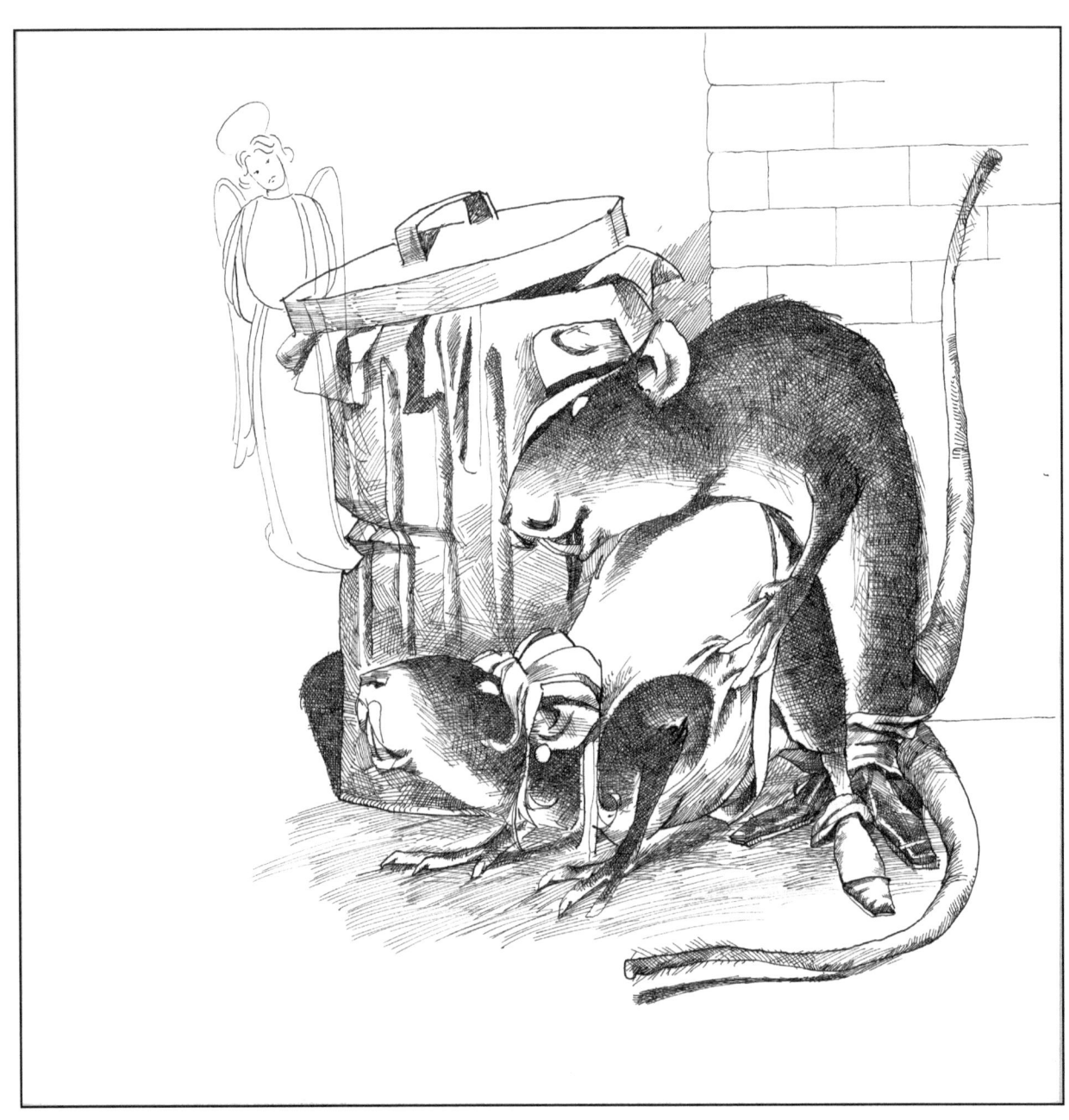

They fell
in love -
Instantly.

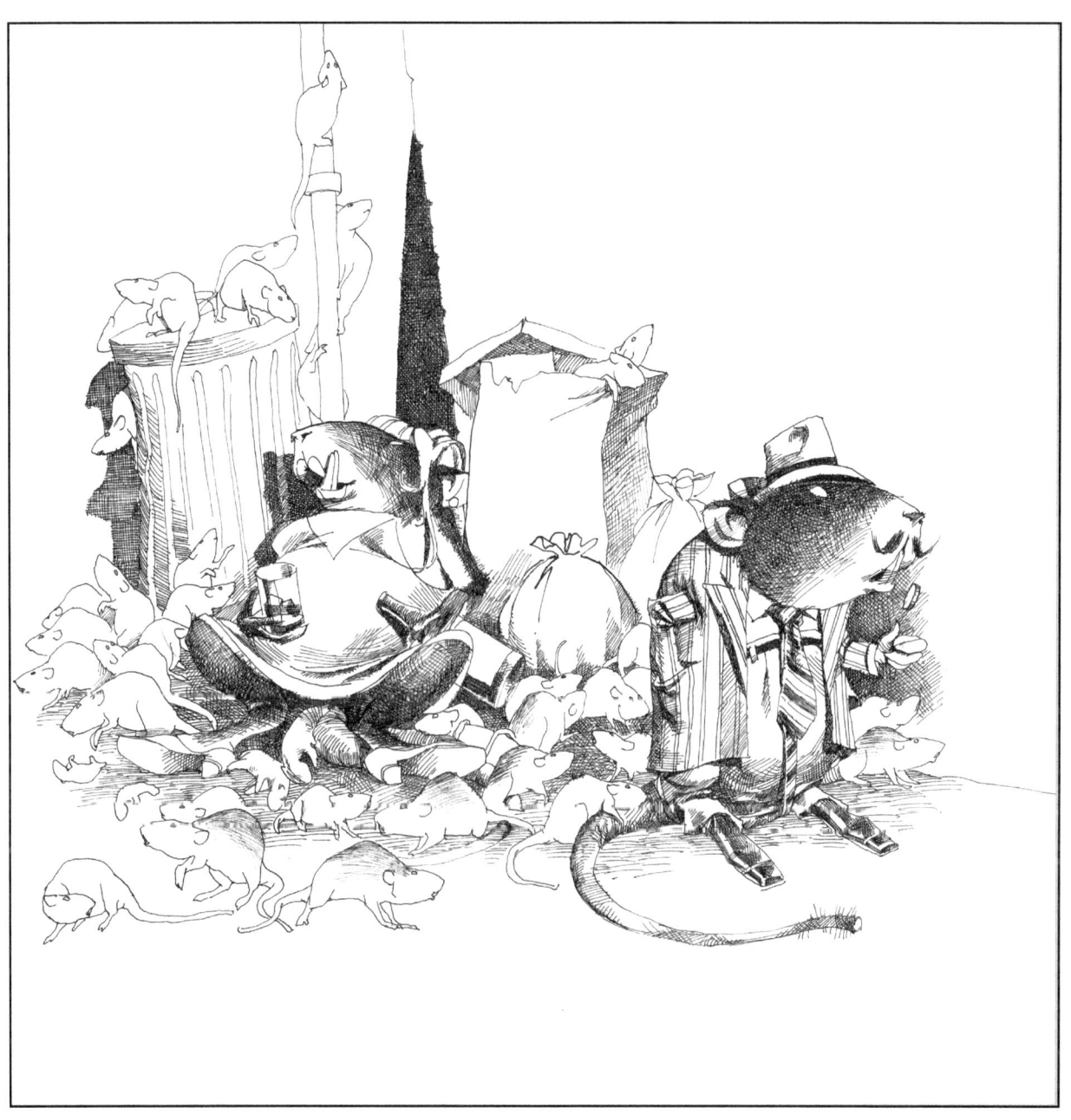

She bore him
many rodents:
One thousand,
seven hundred
and sixty two.

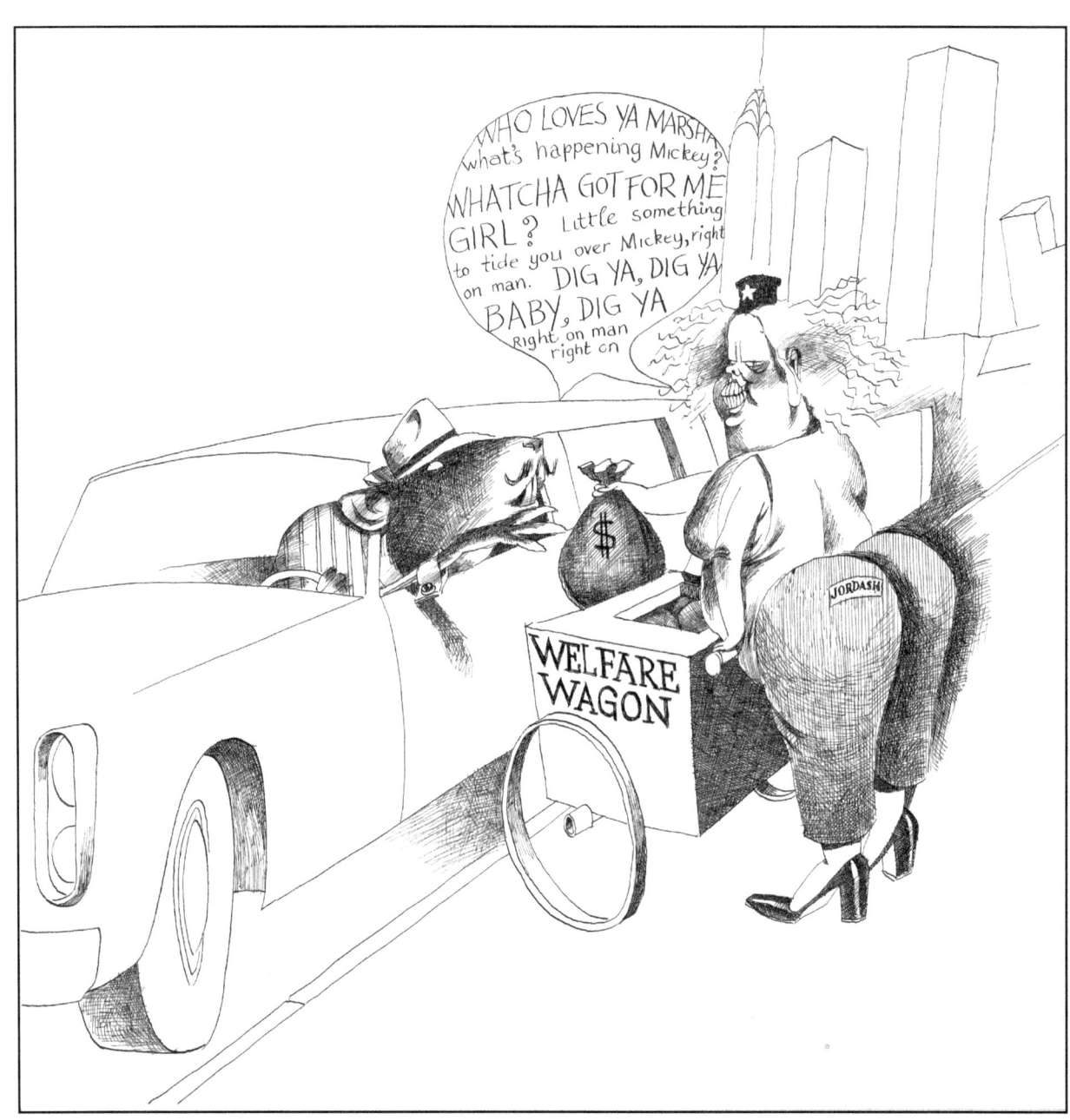

Mickey
went on
welfare.

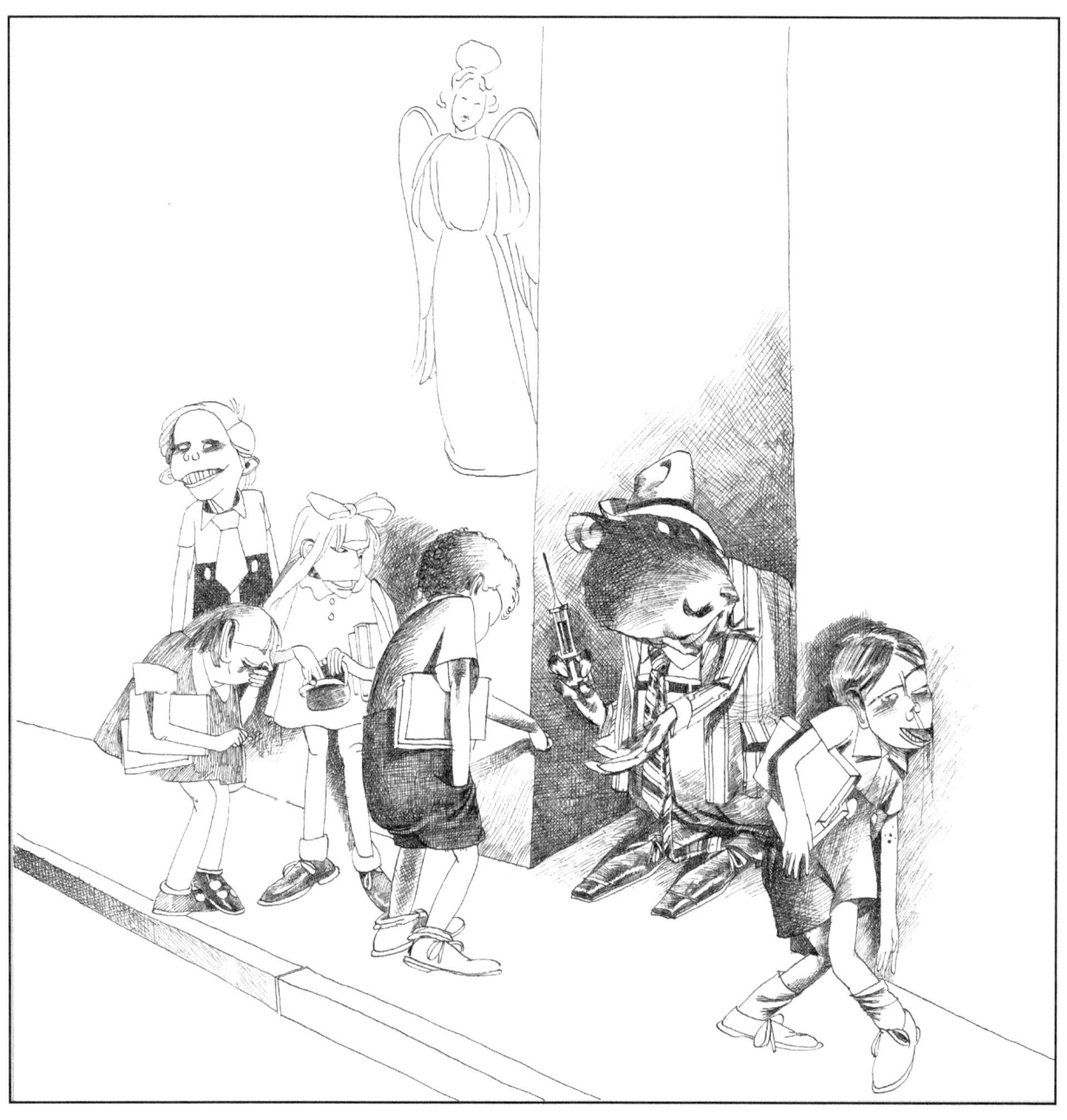

Opened
a small
business.

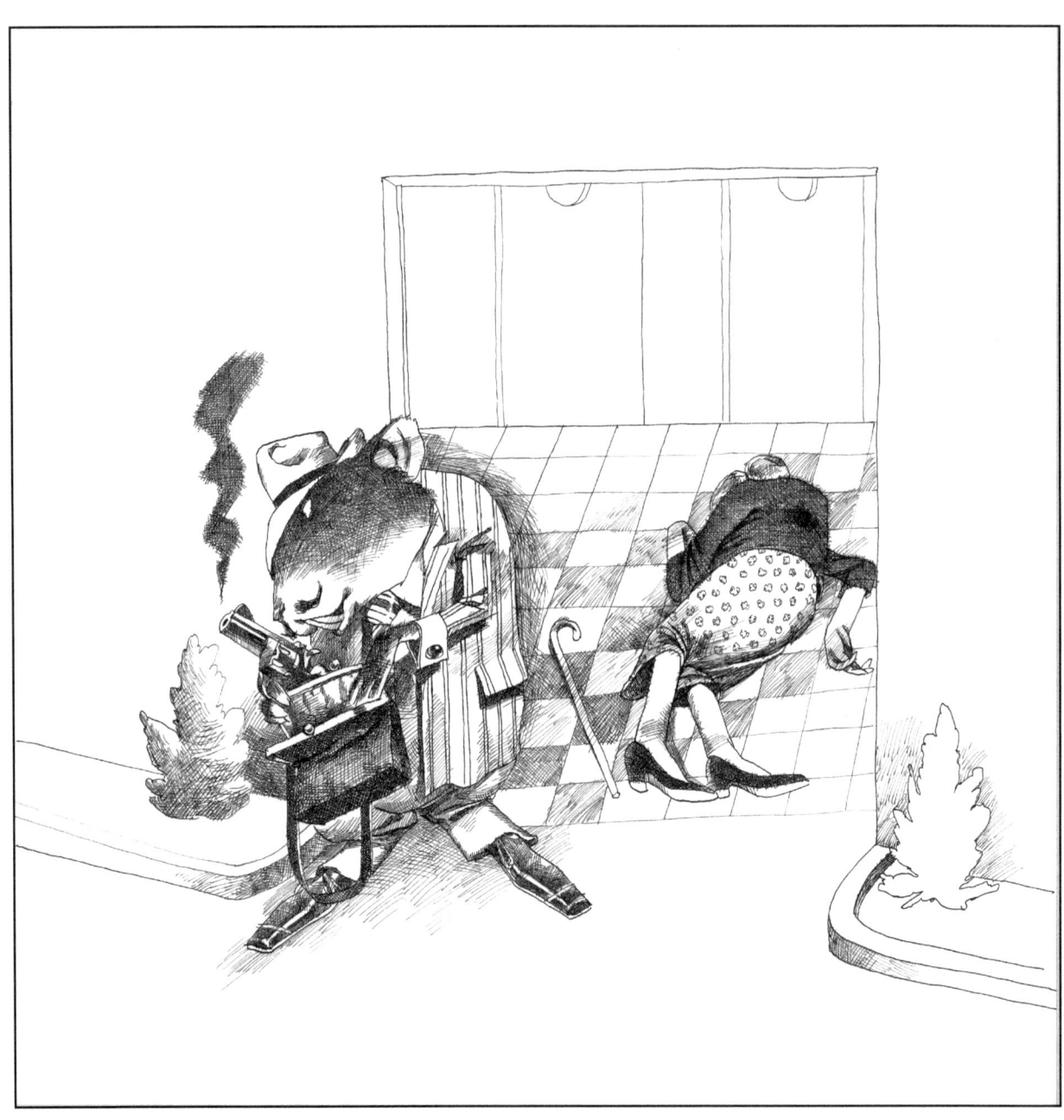

and diversified.

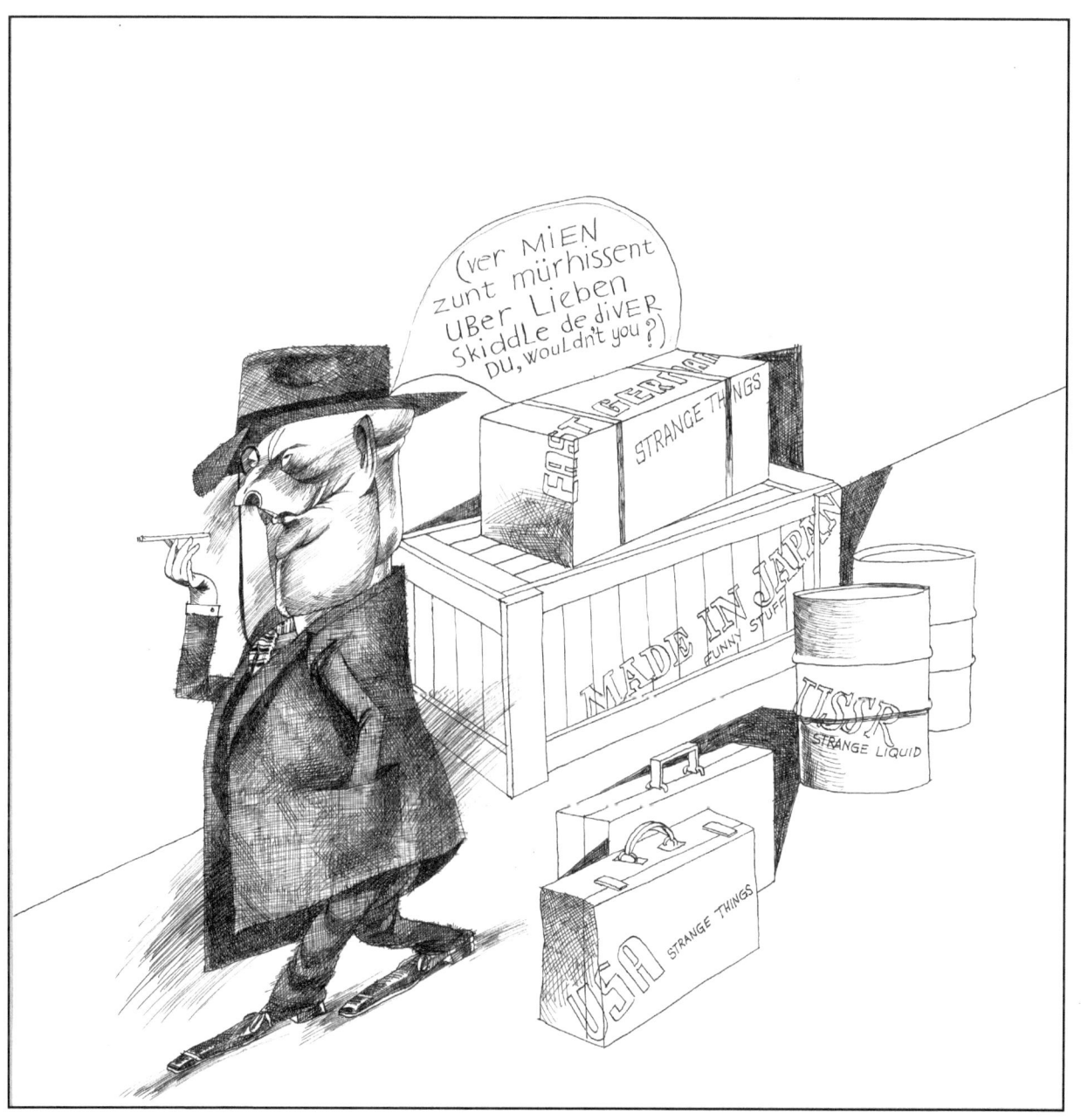

Otto von Klinker, of
Germanic, Asian, and
mechanical
extraction,
considered himself
superior. He was.

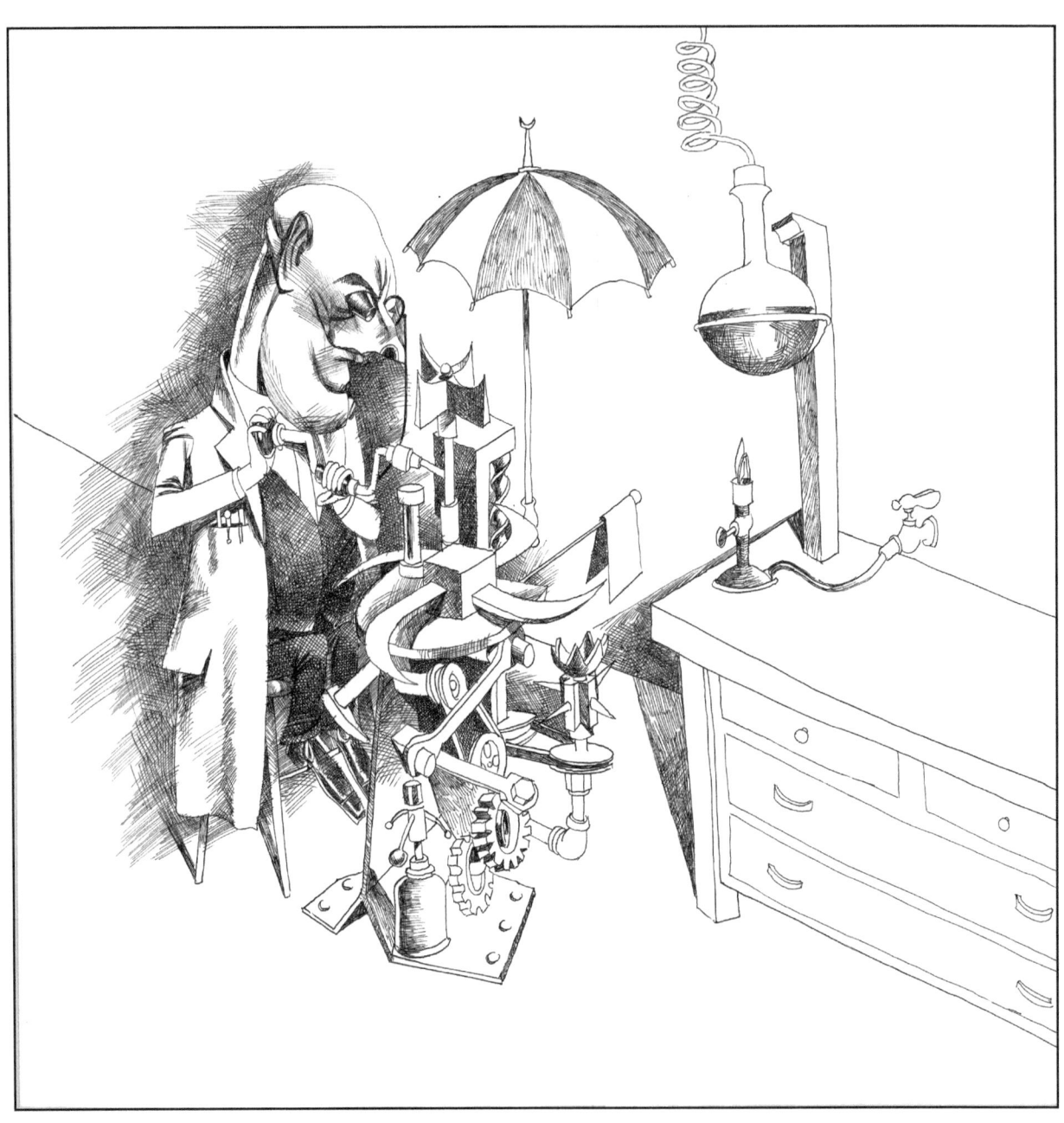

He invented things,
strange things.

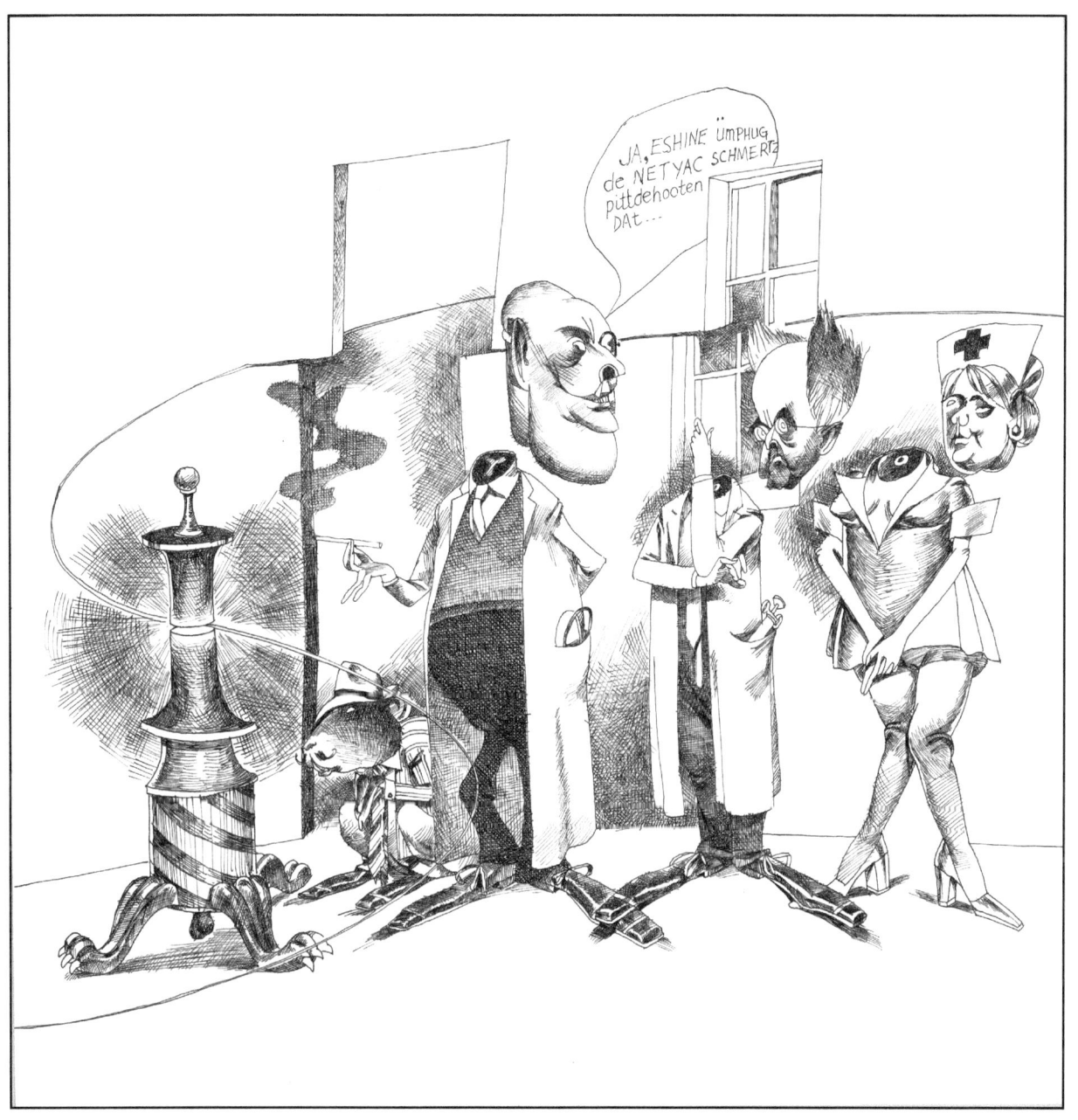

One thing severed
the heads of everything
over six inches high,
including his own.

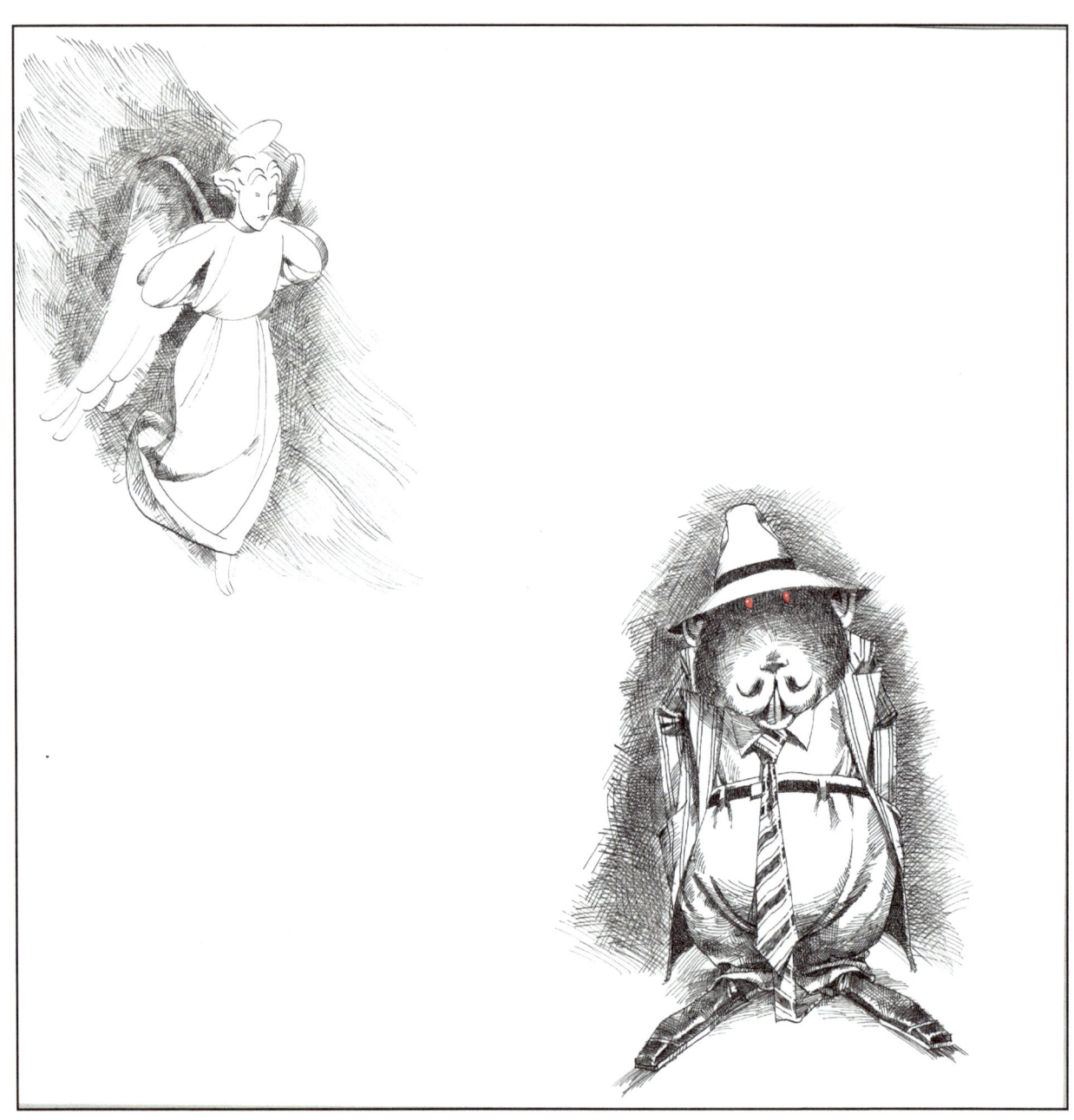

Did this mean that Mickey
would inherit the earth?

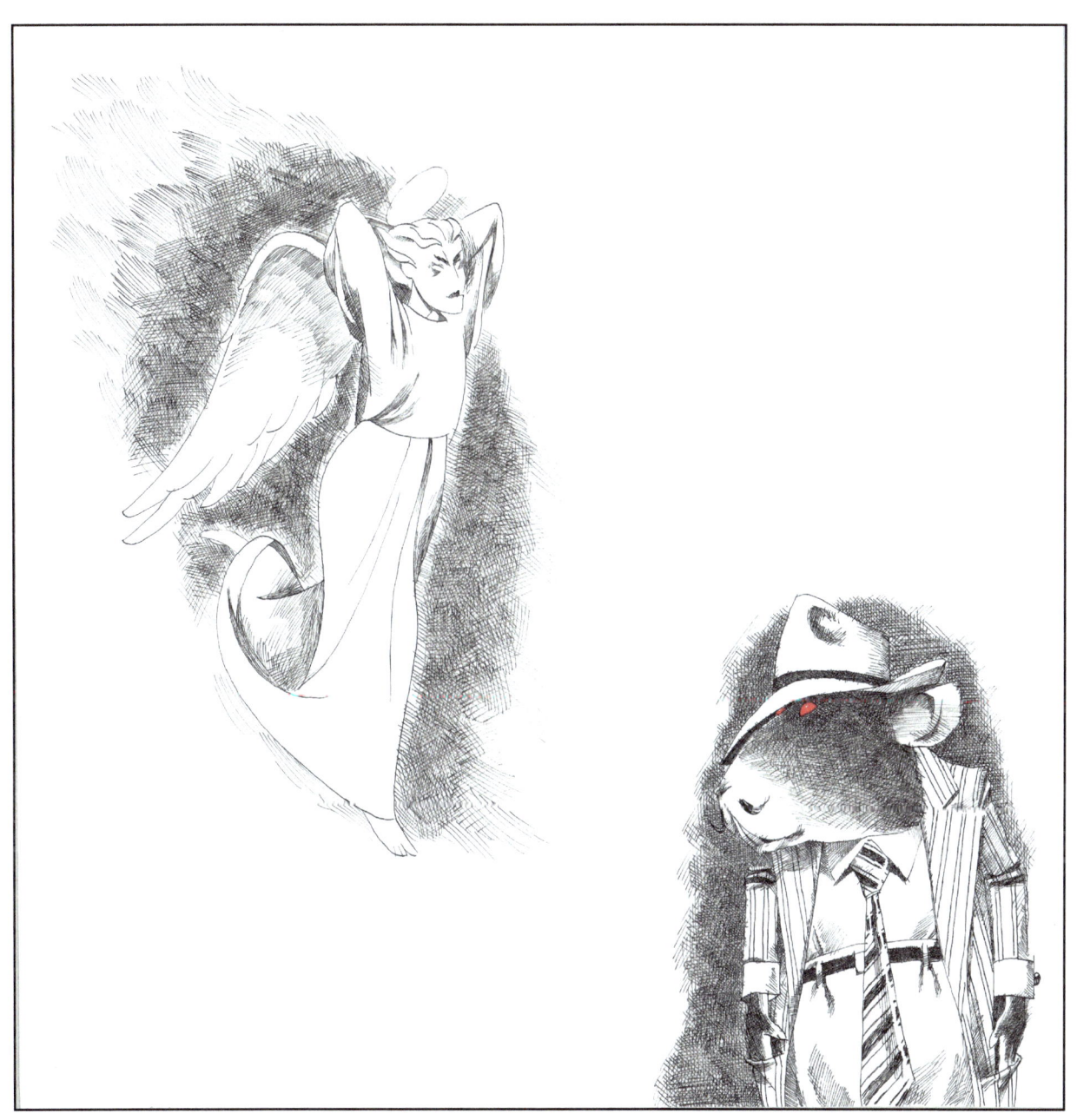

Enter the Angel ot Justice.

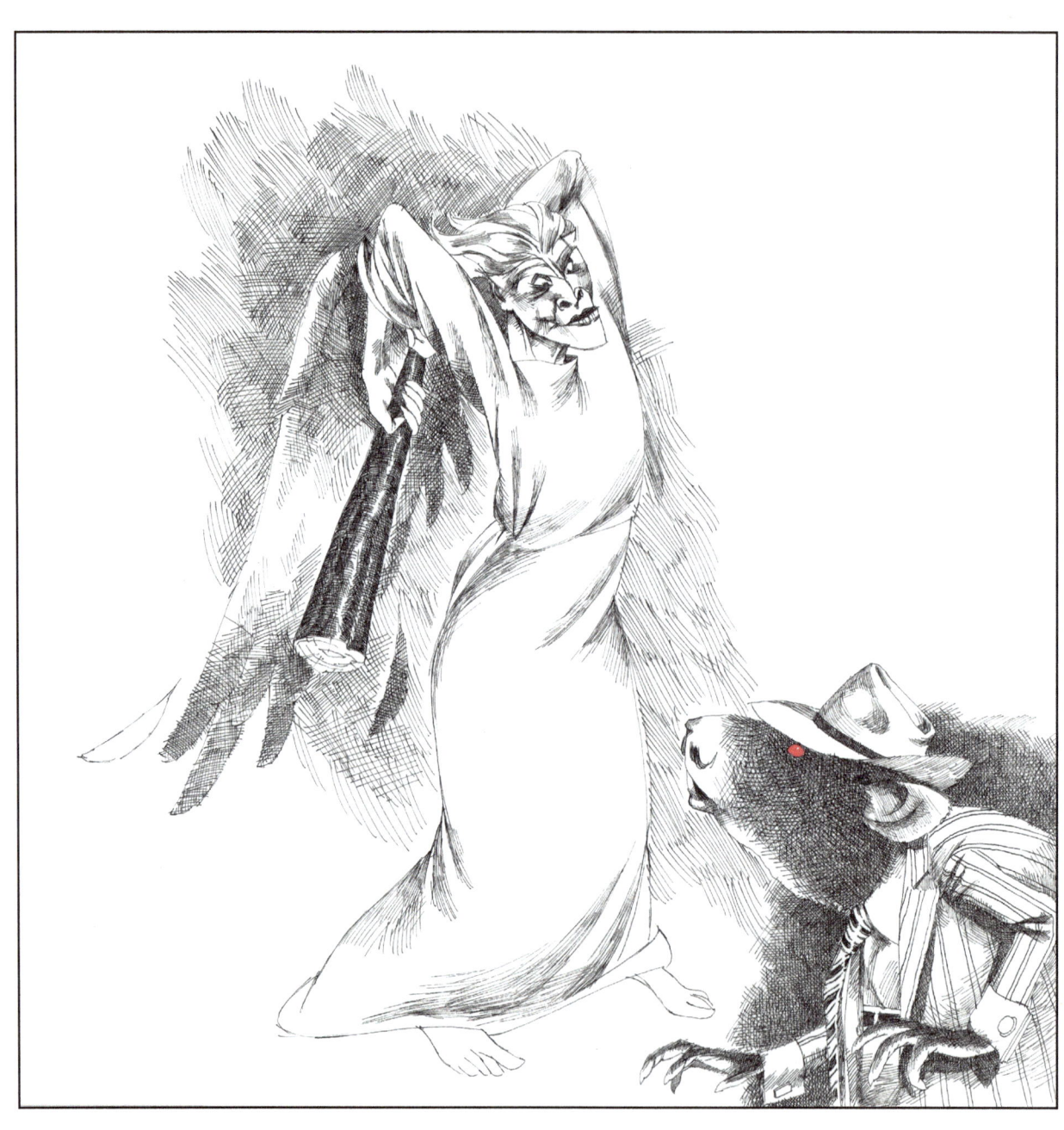

LOOK OUT MICKEY!

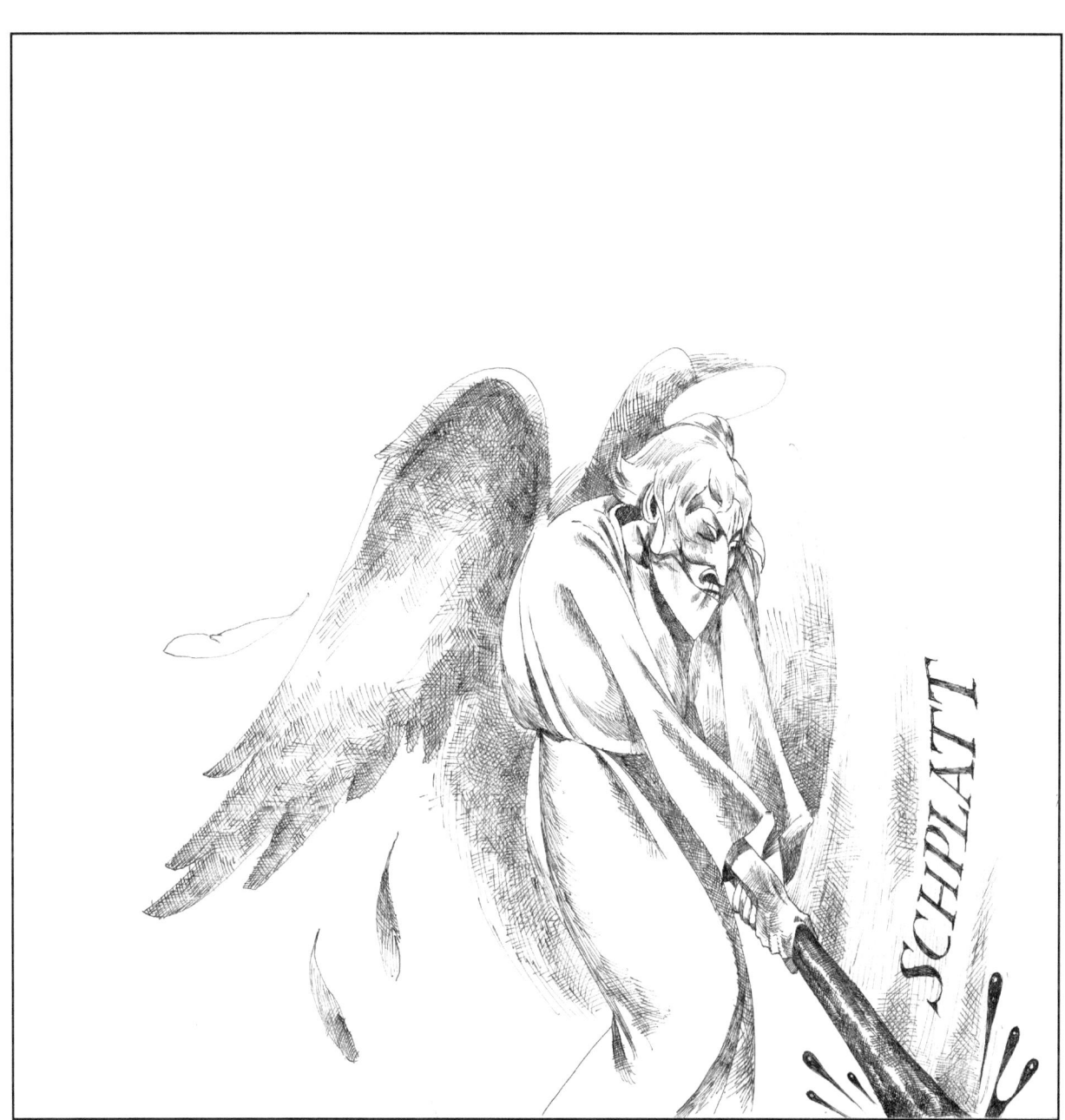

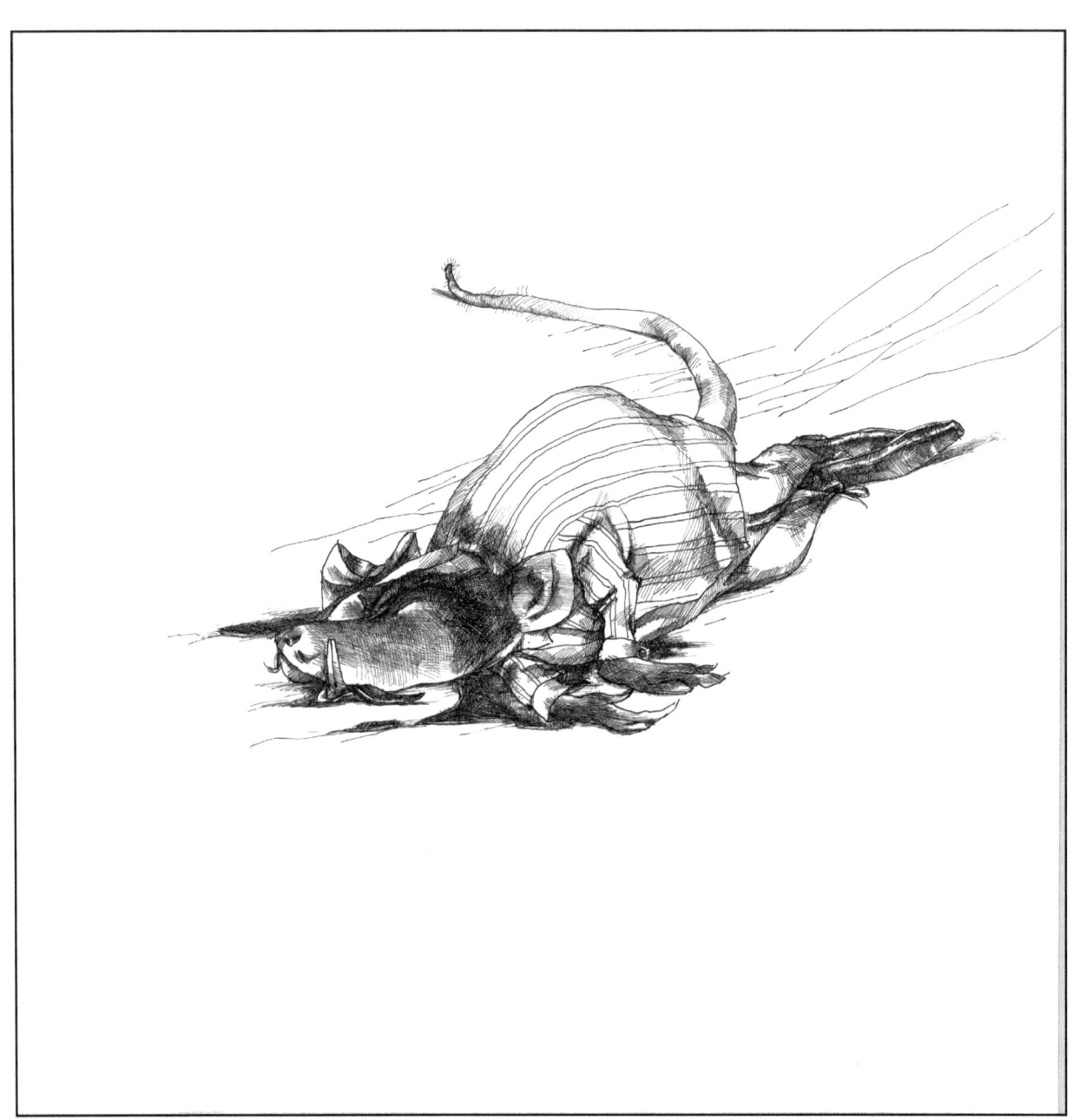

THROUGHOUT THE UNIVERSE,
WE ARE TOLD, THERE ARE
INNUMERABLE BLACK HOLES
FROM WHICH NOTHING ESCAPES

OTHER BOOKS by EDWARD HENRION   (available on amazon.com)

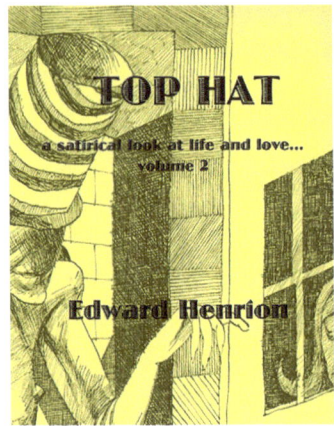

Top Hat: a satirical look at life and love, volume 1
2011

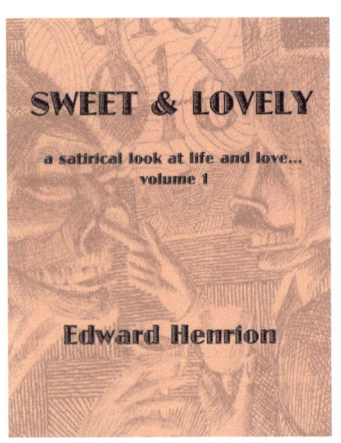

Sweet & Lovely: a satirical look at life and love, volume 2
2011

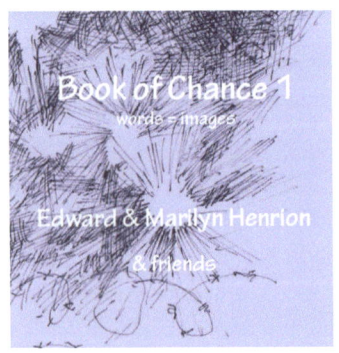

Book of Chance 1
2007

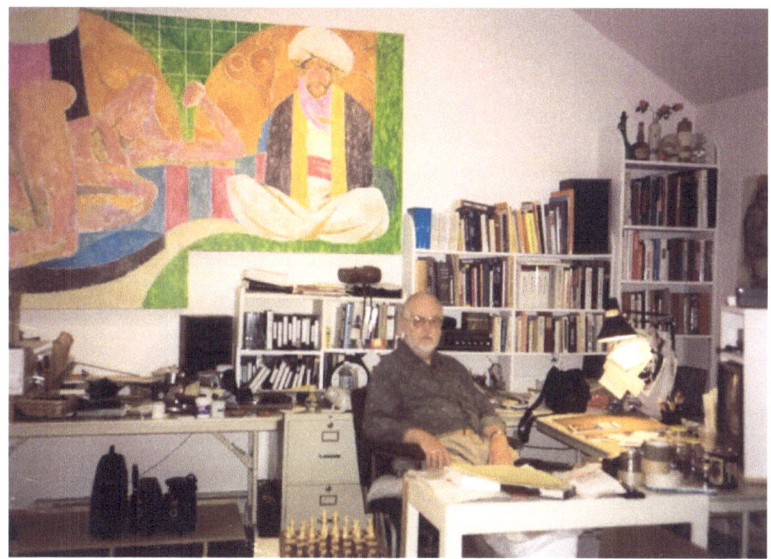

Edward Henrion in his studio circa 1996

BIOGRAPHY

Born in 1928, Ed Henrion grew up in Detroit Michigan. After studying painting with Alexander Zlatov- Mirsky in Chicago, he moved to New York in 1948 where he studied philosophy at Fordham University and graduated from the Cooper Union College of Arts & Sciences in 1952. He lived in Greenwich Village with his wife and fellow Cooper Union graduate, Marilyn Henrion, for over 65 years until his death in 2016. During the 1950's Ed was a regular attendee at the 8th Street Artists' Club, along with the major abstract expressionist painters Motherwell, deKooning, Rothko, Barnett Newman, etc. During the 1960's and 70's the Henrions were immersed in the the art and literary scene of the time. Their social network included Joseph Cornell, Tom Wesselman, and Claes Oldenburg, in whose Happenings Marilyn performed. Salons held at their Greenwich Village apartment featured poetry readings by important poets of the day such as Howard Hart, Allen Ginsberg, Philip Lamantia, Bob Nichols, and Ray Bremser, as well as performances by avant garde composer, Jackson Maclow. Ed's satirical drawings constitute a no-holds-barred commentary on the New York scene and world events as he experienced them during a significant era. The softer side of his nature was manifested in his exquisitely executed nude life drawings and paintings. However, except for occasional freelance editorial illustrations for publications such as *Human Events* and *Libertarian Review,* he studiously avoided any involvement in the business of art. Instead, while continuing to create new drawings and paintings, Ed earned his living as an art teacher at Erasmus High School in Brooklyn, New York before retiring in 1987. He gave up making art in the early '90's and became an avid chess player and science enthusiast.

www.ingramcontent.com/pod-product-compliance
Lightning Source LLC
Chambersburg PA
CBHW041307180526
45172CB00003B/1005